JESUS' FINAL WEEK

CINDY BUNCH

8 STUDIES
FOR INDIVIDUALS
OR GROUPS

ivp

Life
Builder
Study

INTER-VARSITY PRESS
36 Causton Street, London SW1P 4ST, England
Email: ivp@ivpbooks.com
Website: www.ivpbooks.com

Studies 1 and 7 are adapted from the LifeBuilder Bible Study *Matthew*, revised edition © 2000 by Stephen and Jacalyn Eyre, used with permission of InterVarsity Press.
Studies 2 and 5 are adapted from the LifeBuilder Bible Study *Mark*, revised edition © 1999 by James Hoover, used with permission of InterVarsity Press.
Studies 3 and 4 are adapted from the LifeBuilder Bible Study *Meeting Jesus*, revised edition © Leighton Ford, used with permission of InterVarsity Press.
Study 6 is adapted from the LifeBuilder Bible Study *John* by Douglas Connelly, © 1990, used with permission of InterVarsity Press.
Study 8 is adapted from the LifeBuilder Bible Study *Jesus the Reason* by James W. Sire, third edition © 1996, used with permission of InterVarsity Press.

Originally published in the United States of America in the LifeGuide® Bible Studies series in 2000 by InterVarsity Press, Downers Grove, Illinois
First published in Great Britain by Scripture Union in 2000
This edition published in Great Britain by Inter-Varsity Press 2019

British Library Cataloguing-in-Publication Data
A catalogue record for this book is available from the British Library.

ISBN: 978-1-78359-864-9

Printed in Great Britain by Ashford Colour Press Ltd, Gosport, Hampshire

Inter-Varsity Press publishes Christian books that are true to the Bible and that communicate the gospel, develop discipleship and strengthen the church for its mission in the world.

IVP originated within the Inter-Varsity Fellowship, now the Universities and Colleges Christian Fellowship, a student movement connecting Christian Unions in universities and colleges throughout Great Britain, and a member movement of the International Fellowship of Evangelical Students. Website: www.uccf.org.uk. That historic association is maintained, and all senior IVP staff and committee members subscribe to the UCCF Basis of Faith.

Contents

Getting the Most
Out of *Jesus' Final Week*

Once every year the church calendar calls us to walk through the events of the final week of Jesus' life. We celebrate Palm Sunday with exuberance. We weep through Good Friday. We eagerly await Easter day.

Many of the events of this final week will be familiar to you. But you may find it helpful to study them in order, gaining a bit of perspective from each of the four Gospel writers. You'll end up with a more well-rounded perspective of what God was doing in that week that changed our world.

These studies will be of great benefit to you any time. But you may want to give special consideration to using them during your preparation for Easter. In some church traditions we prepare for Easter all in the space of one packed week. In other traditions a Lenten period of quiet reflection begins forty days earlier with Ash Wednesday observations. Whichever your tradition, this guide can be a resource for you. You can go through one study a week on your own or in a small group during the weeks of Lent. Or you can go through a study each day the week before Easter to prepare for the glorious day of resurrection.

As you look at the contents page, you'll note that there are no studies for Wednesday or Saturday. Wednesday appears to be a day of rest for Jesus—no biblical events are recorded. Likewise, there are no texts describing what Saturday, the day between crucifixion and resurrection, was like. Thursday is split into two studies as there's much ground to cover. And the final study begins a new week—celebrating the resurrection.

May you gain insight and wisdom from following the path to the cross—the path that Jesus, King of all kings and Suffering Servant, walked for us.

Suggestions for Individual Study

1. As you begin each study, pray that God will speak to you through his Word.

2. Read the introduction to the study and respond to the personal reflection question or exercise. This is designed to help you focus on God and on the theme of the study.

3. Each study deals with a particular passage—so that you can delve into the author's meaning in that context. Read and reread the passage to be studied. The questions are written using the language of the New International Version, so you may wish to use that version of the Bible. The New Revised Standard Version is also recommended.

4. This is an inductive Bible study, designed to help you discover for yourself what Scripture is saying. The study includes three types of questions. *Observation* questions ask about the basic facts: who, what, when, where and how. *Interpretation* questions delve into the meaning of the passage. *Application* questions help you discover the implications of the text for growing in Christ. These three keys unlock the treasures of Scripture.

Write your answers to the questions in the spaces provided or in a personal journal. Writing can bring clarity and deeper understanding of yourself and of God's Word.

5. It might be good to have a Bible dictionary handy. Use it to look up any unfamiliar words, names or places.

6. Use the prayer suggestion to guide you in thanking God for what you have learned and to pray about the applications that have come to mind.

7. You may want to go on to the suggestion under "Now or Later," or you may want to use that idea for your next study.

Suggestions for Members of a Group Study

1. Come to the study prepared. Follow the suggestions for individual study mentioned above. You will find that careful preparation will greatly enrich your time spent in group discussion.

2. Be willing to participate in the discussion. The leader of your group will not be lecturing. Instead, he or she will be encouraging the members of the group to discuss what they have learned. The leader will be asking the questions that are found in this guide.

3. Stick to the topic being discussed. Your answers should be based on the verses which are the focus of the discussion and not on outside authorities such as commentaries or speakers. These studies focus on a particular passage of Scripture. Only rarely should you refer to other portions of the Bible. This allows for everyone to participate in in-depth study on equal ground.

4. Be sensitive to the other members of the group. Listen attentively when they describe what they have learned. You may be surprised by their insights! Each question assumes a variety of answers. Many questions do not have "right" answers, particularly questions that aim at meaning or application. Instead the questions push us to explore the passage more thoroughly.

When possible, link what you say to the comments of others. Also, be affirming whenever you can. This will encourage some of the more hesitant members of the group to participate.

5. Be careful not to dominate the discussion. We are sometimes so eager to express our thoughts that we leave too little opportunity for others to respond. By all means participate! But allow others to also.

6. Expect God to teach you through the passage being discussed and through the other members of the group. Pray that you will have an enjoyable and profitable time together, but also that as a result of the study you will find ways that you can take action individually and/or as a group.

7. Remember that anything said in the group is considered confidential and should not be discussed outside the group unless specific permission is given to do so.

8. If you are the group leader, you will find additional suggestions at the back of the guide.

1

Sunday:
Triumphal Entry

Matthew 21:1-11

Remember Milli Vanilli, the eighties pop sensation? They were at the top of the charts . . . until it was discovered that their singers were lip-syncing. Remember Cabbage Patch Dolls? They were another eighties sensation that came and went one Christmas season. Popular acclaim can be fickle.

GROUP DISCUSSION. What are some short-lived trends you recall? Think about music, fashion, books and toys.

PERSONAL REFLECTION. What draws people into following the latest trends?

In Matthew 21 Jesus' popularity reaches its zenith. In the midst of public acclamation he "occupies" Jerusalem, the capital of the Jewish nation. As Jesus enters Jerusalem during Passover Week, excitement is building and emotions are intense. *Read Matthew 21:1-11.*

---

1. Identify words or phrases that communicate something of the electrifying atmosphere in the city.

2. What might the disciples have thought and felt when they heard Jesus' instructions in verses 2-3?

3. How do you think you would have responded to such instructions from Jesus?

4. Notice the prophecy in verse 5. What various levels of significance do you see in Jesus' riding on a donkey?

5. How is honor given to Jesus in verses 7-11?

---

6. What different perceptions does the crowd have of Jesus?

---

7. Describe a time when you have been swept up in a public celebration of Jesus.

What factors made this time significant?

How did it affect you?

8. As you begin this study of Jesus' final week, how would you like your worship to be transformed?

9. When you think of all the trends that come and go, what does it mean to you to worship the Christ who stands beyond time?

Praise and celebrate the donkey-riding Christ who has come to be our King.

Now or Later

In the next study we will see Jesus enter the temple with authority and deal with sin. To prepare for that study, imagine your heart as a temple into which Jesus walks, looking for the fruit of prayer. As he looks around, what does he see, and then what does he say to you? Spend time with this image and use it as a means of conversational prayer with God. Ask him what he would like you to do to begin to be more fruitful. Ask him where you can find fertilizer. Ask him what weeds need to be pulled out.

2

Monday: Clearing the Temple

Mark 11:12-19

The trouble with righteous anger is that it is so much easier to be angry than righteous. But it is possible to be both.

GROUP DISCUSSION. How would you define righteous anger? When have you seen it put to good use?

PERSONAL REFLECTION. When has anger gotten the better of you lately? Ask God to help you discern the real cause of the anger.

Jesus well illustrates righteous anger in this passage. He also suggests that even righteous anger must be joined with prayer and forgiveness. This passage provides an example of how our emotions and attitudes can work toward God's purposes instead of against them. *Read Mark 11:12-19.*

---

1. How would you have felt if you had been a witness to the events of this passage?

2. How do the events in this passage compare or contrast with the events of the previous study?

3. What was Jesus trying to communicate when he cursed the fig tree (v. 14)?

4. Put yourself in Jesus' place. Why is he so angry about what is taking place in the temple (vv. 15-17)?

5. In what ways would Jesus' anger in this situation qualify as righteous anger?

6. Compare and contrast the response of the chief priests and the teachers with that of the crowd (v. 18).

What do you think is the reason for their different responses?

---

7. What activities of Christians in the world today might arouse God's anger?

---

8. Now make it personal. What activities or attitudes in your church or fellowship get in the way of God's purposes?

What can you do to help eliminate them?

---

9. When you react to a situation with anger, how can you know whether that anger is from God or not?

Confess any sins of anger that you may have become aware of. Ask God to use you as a tool for his justice.

Now or Later

10. *Read Mark 11:20-25.* Why do you suppose Mark has sandwiched this account of Jesus' clearing of the temple within that of the cursing of the fig tree?

11. What kind of fruit was Jesus looking for in Israel?

12. Many people believe they will escape the judgment of God simply because they are religious. How can this passage serve as a warning to them and to us?

13. Are there people you are holding ungodly anger against? Begin to pray about this, and plan appropriate action steps as a Lenten discipline.

3

Tuesday:
Teaching at
the Mount of Olives

Matthew 24:1-31

The Chinese have a proverb: "Prophesying is always very diffi-cult, especially about the future!" In the Bible, prophecy is not only knowledge of the future but insight into the present. In Mat-thew 24 we see Jesus the prophet—and a very realistic prophet. His picture of what lies ahead is not of a world where everything will get better and better. He does not begin to suggest that every-one will eagerly embrace his cause or his followers.

GROUP DISCUSSION. Why do you think so many people are fas-cinated with prophecy—biblical and otherwise?

PERSONAL REFLECTION. If you could ask for a prophecy about your own life, what would you want to know about: what career to choose? if and whom you will marry? how God will call you to serve him?

False prophets tell us what we *want* to hear. True prophets tell us what we *need* to hear. We would like Jesus to be the great positive thinker. Yet he came not only to bring peace to the troubled but trouble to those who are being lulled into a false peace. *Read Matthew 24:1-31.*

---

1. If you were a reporter assigned to cover Jesus' speech, what would be your headline?

---

2. The disciples asked, "When?" (v. 3). Why do you think Jesus did not answer them more directly?

---

3. In verses 4 and 5 Jesus warns his disciples about being deceived. What are some of the marks of a deceiver (see 1 John 4:1-6)?

---

4. In what ways do you think people today are being deceived?

In what areas are you vulnerable to deceit?

---

5. Jesus sees human history as being very unstable (vv. 6-8). What signs of instability does he mention?

How are these signs like "the beginning of birth pains" (v. 8)?

---

6. What will happen to Jesus' disciples and to others as the end approaches (vv. 9-13)?

What does it mean for us to "stand firm" (v. 13) during such times?

7. When the "abomination that causes desolation" comes, what actions should believers take, and why (vv. 15-22)?

8. As Jesus' followers watch for his return during those days, how can they tell the difference between false Christs and the true one (vv. 23-31)?

9. How can we "keep watch" and "be ready" for Jesus?

What spiritual disciplines are you (or would you like to be) incorporating into your life to help you watch for Jesus?

Ask God to give you clarity in reading the "signs of the times" and to guide you in being prepared for his return.

Now or Later

10. *Read Matthew 24:32-51.* How can we apply the lesson of the fig tree (vv. 32-35) to the events preceding Christ's return?

_____

11. How will the coming of Christ be like the days of Noah (vv. 36-41)?

_____

12. What do the stories of the homeowner and the servants teach us about the Lord's return (vv. 42-51)?

_____

13. When is it hard for you to trust in the Lord's return?

Tell Jesus you trust him to save you from judgment in the last days—whether your trust is large or little for now. A small amount of faith (trust) goes a long way in the kingdom.

4

Thursday: The Last Supper

A crisis reveals what kind of people we are. Some people crumble and give up in the face of a crisis. Some people deny that the crisis exists. Some people blame others for the crisis. A few people rise up to meet the crisis, doing more than anyone else in the same position is able to do.

GROUP DISCUSSION. How do you typically respond in a crisis, and why?

PERSONAL REFLECTION. Think of what you've learned about Jesus. Have you seen him encounter crises? How did he respond? How do you think he will respond to the crisis that will end his earthly life?

In Matthew 26 the hostility that began early in Jesus' ministry approaches a violent end. Yet although he awaits his arrest and crucifixion, he is magnificently in control. *He* plans the last meal. *He* knows who will betray him. *He* offers himself as a sacrifice. When we—like Jesus—are doing the Father's will, even the inevitabilities of sin, suffering and death lose their power to imprison us. Here the victim is the one who is most free! *Read Matthew 26:17-30.*

---

1. Classical art and modern communion services have probably influenced your picture of this event. Now that you have the text fresh in your mind, how would you describe the setting of this passage?

---

2. What was the significance of the "Passover" (v. 17; see Exodus 12:1-29)?

---

3. What irony do you see in the disciples' making preparation for Jesus to eat the Passover (v. 17; see Mark 14:12; 1 Corinthians 5:7)?

---

4. Jesus is often portrayed as a wonderful teacher but an ultimately helpless martyr. What words and acts show him to be very much in control (vv. 18-25; see also Mark 14:13-16)?

How did he show extraordinary knowledge and insight?

5. Describe what happened when Jesus told the disciples that one of them would betray him (v. 22).

6. Do you ever wonder if you are going to betray Jesus—or if you will rise up to meet the crisis? Explain.

7. What does verse 24 tell us about God's will and human responsibility?

8. What does the Lord's Supper teach us about the meaning of Jesus' death (vv. 26-29)?

9. What can we infer from the Lord's Supper about the kind of response we need to make in order to benefit from his death?

10. It is a wonderful privilege to be able to re-create this event with other believers. When have you found the Lord's Supper particularly meaningful?

What are the particular elements that make it meaningful?

11. How can sharing the Lord's Supper together make us ready to face the crises of life?

Ask the living Christ to guide you through a crisis you may be facing. Coming face to face with Jesus will show you what kind of person you are. If you can say it and mean it, tell Jesus you appreciate the crisis he faced for you, and ask him to help you to change to be more like him.

Now or Later

12. *Read Matthew 26:6-13.* To some, the woman's pouring of costly perfume was a waste (vv. 6-13). To Jesus, it was beautiful. When can extravagance be beautiful?

13. What factors justified the woman's extravagance?

14. In what ways should we be extravagant in our worship of Jesus?

5

Thursday: Betrayal & Arrest

Mark 14:43-72

The persecution of enemies is one thing, the abandonment of friends another. The former we expect. The latter always catches us off guard. Those who are close to us have the power to hurt us in deep, personal ways that others do not.

GROUP DISCUSSION. What does being loyal to a friend mean to you?

PERSONAL REFLECTION. What pressures in your life test your loyalty to Jesus Christ? Tell him what you are feeling.

In this study we find Jesus not only betrayed by one of his disciples but abandoned by all the others and denied by one of his closest friends. All this added to the cruel and unlawful treatment by the Sanhedrin. This account reveals how intense pressures can test the quality of our discipleship. *Read Mark 14:43-72.*

1. What mixed motives do you see among the main characters in this passage?

2. In particular, what mixed motives may have inspired Judas's words and action of betrayal (vv. 43-45)?

3. How does Jesus respond to his betrayal?

4. The unnamed young man (vv. 51-52) seems symbolic of all Jesus' followers. How does his predicament reflect Jesus' earlier warnings about the cost of discipleship (Mark 8:34-38)?

5. What aspects of Jesus' trial before the Sanhedrin does Mark emphasize?

6. Up until this point Jesus has regularly withheld his identity, but in verse 62 he openly confesses his identity as the Christ. Why do you think he does so now?

7. How is the charge against Jesus (v. 64) both justifiable and unjustifiable?

8. What traits or actions of Jesus, in contrast to his disciples, are an example of what he desires his followers to be like (vv. 55-65)?

9. What mix of motives brings Peter into the high priest's courtyard yet keeps him from acknowledging his relationship to Jesus (vv. 66-72)?

10. How are your motives mixed in following Jesus?

11. How is Judas's betrayal of Jesus different from Peter's?

12. In what circumstances are you most tempted to be ashamed of Jesus or to deny him?

13. What warnings and encouragement can you draw from Peter's experience?

Ask the Lord to sort out your motives and to help you be faithful to him.

Now or Later

Read Mark 14:32-42. In verse 34 and again in verse 38 Jesus encourages the disciples to watch and pray so that they will not fall into temptation. What particular temptations were they about to face?

How might prayer have changed the outcome?

How might these same exhortations make the difference in your own life between resisting and falling into temptation?

What can you do to ensure that the next weeks are a time for you to "watch and pray"?

6

Friday: Trial

"Christ Killers!" The words made my stomach tighten. Someone had spray-painted the words and a series of swastikas on the Jewish synagogue in our city. Anti-Semitism had raised its ugly head again. Unfortunately, Nazism is just one example of ways in which people have used the Christian faith to support their own belief systems.

GROUP DISCUSSION. What are some other historical and current ways in which the message of Christianity is being distorted to fit a particular ideology?

PERSONAL REFLECTION. What temptation to compromise your faith do you face? Ask the one who has faced trial in Pilate's court to give you strength.

The New Testament does blame the Jewish leaders for condemning Jesus to die. But they weren't acting alone. The Roman governor Pontius Pilate also condemned Jesus to die. We meet Pilate in this study. *Read John 18:28—19:16.*

1. What do you notice about Pilate as you read this passage?

2. How do the Jewish leaders reveal their hypocrisy by refusing to enter the home of Pilate, a Gentile (18:28)?

———————————————————————————

3. A Roman trial included four basic elements: the accusation, the interrogation (search for evidence), the defense, and the verdict. What events or statements from the text are included in each?

☐ the accusation (18:28-31)

☐ the interrogation (18:32-35)

☐ the defense (18:36-37)

☐ the verdict (18:38)

---

4. Pilate's statement "What is truth?" (18:38) seems strikingly current. How do you find yourself confronted by unbelievers with this question?

---

5. Pilate obviously was trying to release Jesus. What specific attempts did he make (18:39—19:16)?

---

6. How does it make you feel when you read the record of injustice done toward Jesus?

7. What can you conclude about Pilate's character after reading this passage?

8. The Jews' true charge against Jesus comes out in 19:7—"He claimed to be the Son of God." Why do you think Pilate reacted to that statement as he did (19:8-9)?

9. Why didn't Jesus say more to Pilate (19:9-11)?

10. What parallels can you draw between the crowd's threats toward Pilate (19:12) and the world's attempts to detour Christians from fully following Christ?

11. The message of the gospel is that Jesus took upon himself the condemnation that we deserve. In what specific ways do you see Christ's grace demonstrated in his trial before Pilate?

12. What does this passage tell you about how to respond when you are treated unjustly?

Ask God to help you follow Jesus' example of grace when you are under pressure.

Now or Later

Return to Peter's denial. John's account is in 18:15-18, 25-27. Let this text be a source of prayer and reflection. Imagine yourself in Peter's situation. Who in your world is questioning you about your relationship with Jesus? How do you respond? Ask God to show you if there are ways in which you are denying him.

7

Friday: Crucifixion

Matthew 27

Often our first response to pain is to run from it and deny what we feel, thinking somehow that life is supposed to be easy, smooth and comfortable. In his book *The Road Less Traveled* Scott Peck opens up new levels of personal growth for many by challenging his readers to admit, "Life is difficult." Peck goes on to say that most emotional disorders come from the illegitimate avoidance of suffering. Because Jesus taught, "Blessed are those who mourn, for they shall be comforted," Christians can say that honestly facing and feeling our grief is the best way through it.

GROUP DISCUSSION. In what specific ways might helping a person mourn in the midst of pain be a better approach than telling someone to "cheer up" or to "keep a stiff upper lip"?

How have you been encouraged or discouraged by others in times of personal grief and loss?

PERSONAL REFLECTION. Somewhere in our hearts there is pain from loss and grief that we have yet to fully face. Ask God to give you the courage to come into those places of pain so that he can comfort you. Rest for a while in his comforting presence.

Matthew 27 records the execution of Jesus. As Pilate and the religious leaders condemn, mock and crucify God's Son, God himself seems strangely absent. Yet to those who have eyes to see, his presence and power are unmistakable. *Read the entire chapter aloud,* taking turns, with each person reading about ten verses.

---

1. What emotional reactions do you have to this text?

---

2. In what ways and by whom is Jesus mocked (vv. 27-44)?

Why do they mock Jesus?

3. As death begins to engulf him, Jesus cries out to God (vv. 45-46). What do his cry and the overshadowing darkness reveal about his relationship to the Father during this torment?

4. Was it necessary for Jesus to feel that God had forsaken him? Why or why not?

5. As the centurion witnesses the strange events surrounding Jesus' death, he exclaims, "Surely he was the Son of God!" (v. 54). What clues do the unusual events referred to in verses 45-56 provide for understanding the events of this chapter?

6. Observe the role Jesus' followers play during the events of his crucifixion and burial (vv. 55-61). How do you think they felt?

7. Look over the entire chapter again. How is the character of each person revealed as they respond to Jesus in captivity and death?

8. Observe the final measures the chief priests and Pharisees take to insure that their victory over Jesus is complete (vv. 62-66). How does the guarding of the tomb bring together the power of the Romans with the power of the Jews?

9. This chapter is filled with irony. Satan's triumph is actually

his defeat. Christ's "defeat" is actually his triumph. How should this challenge our views about the way God works in our lives?

10. Where in your life do you need hope?

What would it take for you to find that hope in God?

Ask God to give you the faith to face the pain that comes from living in a world that kills its Savior.

Now or Later

Saturday is the missing day in this last week of Jesus' life. It is a day of waiting. In some traditions an Easter vigil is kept in the church. People pray and read Scripture throughout the night, watching for Jesus. Create your own Easter vigil time of prayer and waiting this week as you prepare for Easter.

8

Sunday: Resurrection

Luke 24:1-43

The Easter hymns are some of the most glorious in the Christian tradition: "He lives, he lives, Christ Jesus lives today!" "Christ the Lord is risen today." In some churches the Hallelujah Chorus is sung. We bring out the brass and our best soloists. Our praise teams and choirs have extra rehearsals to learn new music. We come early—just to get a seat—and wear our finest. It is a day of celebration.

GROUP DISCUSSION. What Easter traditions in your church or family have been especially meaningful to you?

PERSONAL REFLECTION. What parts of a worship service most cause you to praise God?

When the apostle Paul mentioned the resurrection of Jesus to the philosophers in Athens, some of them sneered. Some still do. And well they might! After all, such a thing just couldn't happen. Or could it? *Read Luke 24:1-43.*

---

1. Imagine you are returning to the grave of a person you saw buried a few days ago. When you get there you find an open pit and an open casket with no body in it. How would you react?

2. Given the first-century opinion that the testimony of women was not worth much, why do you think Luke mentions them (v. 1)?

3. Why does the first explanation of the empty tomb make sense to the women (vv. 4-7)?

4. What was the reaction of the disciples, Peter in particular (vv. 9-12)?

5. In what ways do you identify with Peter's response?

6. In verses 19-24 what did the two disciples reveal about their hopes for Jesus?

7. Why do you suppose Jesus taught them out of the Old Testament Scriptures (vv. 25-27)?

8. How did the encounter with Jesus affect the two disciples (vv. 31-35)?

9. What evidence for the resurrection is given in verses 37-43?

Of what value is this evidence in the witness of Christ to the world?

Of what value is this evidence in your life?

10. How would you like the fact of the resurrection to shape your daily life?

11. How have you benefited from this series of studies on Jesus' final week?

Christ is risen indeed! Spend time in prayer and praise for this reality.

Now or Later

Lent is a time of intense focus on Jesus. If you have been doing these studies during Lent, you may have had increased spiritual growth or awareness during these past weeks. How will you continue to focus on Jesus in the next weeks and months? Plan for your next group study or quiet-time topic now so that you don't lose momentum.

Leader's Notes

MY GRACE IS SUFFICIENT FOR YOU. (2 COR 12:9)

Leading a Bible discussion can be an enjoyable and rewarding experience. But it can also be *scary*—especially if you've never done it before. If this is your feeling, you're in good company. When God asked Moses to lead the Israelites out of Egypt, he replied, "O Lord, please send someone else to do it"! (Ex 4:13). It was the same with Solomon, Jeremiah and Timothy, but God helped these people in spite of their weaknesses, and he will help you as well.

You don't need to be an expert on the Bible or a trained teacher to lead a Bible discussion. The idea behind these inductive studies is that the leader guides group members to discover for themselves what the Bible has to say. This method of learning will allow group members to remember much more of what is said than a lecture would.

These studies are designed to be led easily. As a matter of fact, the flow of questions through the passage from observation to interpretation to application is so natural that you may feel that the studies lead themselves. This study guide is also flexible. You can use it with a variety of groups—student, professional, neighborhood or church groups. Each study takes forty-five to sixty minutes in a group setting.

There are some important facts to know about group dynamics and encouraging discussion. The suggestions listed below should enable you to effectively and enjoyably fulfill your role as leader.

Preparing for the Study

1. Ask God to help you understand and apply the passage in your own life. Unless this happens, you will not be prepared to lead others. Pray too for the various members of the group. Ask God to open your hearts to the message of his Word and motivate you to action.

2. Read the introduction to the entire guide to get an overview of the entire book and the issues which will be explored.

3. As you begin each study, read and reread the assigned Bible passage to familiarize yourself with it.

4. This study guide is based on the New International Version of the Bible. It will help you and the group if you use this translation as the basis for your study and discussion.

5. Carefully work through each question in the study. Spend time in meditation and reflection as you consider how to respond.

6. Write your thoughts and responses in the space provided in the study guide. This will help you to express your understanding of the passage clearly.

7. It might help to have a Bible dictionary handy. Use it to look up any unfamiliar words, names or places. (For additional help on how to study a passage, see chapter five of *How to Lead a LifeBuilder Study*, IVP, 2018.)

8. Consider how you can apply the Scripture to your life. Remember that the group will follow your lead in responding to the studies. They will not go any deeper than you do.

9. Once you have finished your own study of the passage, familiarize yourself with the leader's notes for the study you are leading. These are designed to help you in several ways. First, they tell you the purpose the study guide author had in mind when writing the study. Take time to think through how the study questions work together to accomplish that purpose. Second, the notes provide you with additional background information or suggestions on group dynamics for various questions. This information can be useful when people have difficulty understanding or answering a question. Third, the leader's notes can alert you to potential problems you may encounter during the study.

10. If you wish to remind yourself of anything mentioned in the leader's notes, make a note to yourself below that question in the study.

Leading the Study

1. Begin the study on time. Open with prayer, asking God to help the group to understand and apply the passage.

2. Be sure that everyone in your group has a study guide. Encourage the group to prepare beforehand for each discussion by reading the introduction to the guide and by working through the questions in the study.

3. At the beginning of your first time together, explain that these studies are meant to be discussions, not lectures. Encourage the members of the group to participate. However, do not put pressure on those who may be hesitant to speak during the first few sessions. You may want to suggest the following guidelines to your group.

☐ Stick to the topic being discussed.

☐ Your responses should be based on the verses which are the focus of the discussion and not on outside authorities such as commentaries or speakers.

☐ These studies focus on a particular passage of Scripture. Only rarely should you refer to other portions of the Bible. This allows for everyone to participate in in-depth study on equal ground.

☐ Anything said in the group is considered confidential and will not be discussed outside the group unless specific permission is given to do so.

☐ We will listen attentively to each other and provide time for each person present to talk.

☐ We will pray for each other.

4. Have a group member read the introduction at the beginning of the discussion.

5. Every session begins with a group discussion question. The question or activity is meant to be used before the passage is read. The question introduces the theme of the study and encourages group members to begin to open up. Encourage as many members as possible to participate, and be ready to get the discussion going with your own response.

This section is designed to reveal where our thoughts or feelings need to be transformed by Scripture. That is why it is especially important not to read the passage before the discussion question is asked. The passage will tend to color the honest reactions people would otherwise give because they are, of course, supposed to think the way the Bible does.

You may want to supplement the group discussion question with an icebreaker to help people to get comfortable. See the community section of the *Small Group Starter Kit* (IVP, 1995) for more ideas.

You also might want to use the personal reflection question with your group. Either allow a time of silence for people to respond individually or discuss it together.

6. Have a group member (or members if the passage is long) read aloud the passage to be studied. Then give people several minutes to read the passage again silently so that they can take it all in.

7. Question 1 will generally be an overview question designed to briefly survey the passage. Encourage the group to look at the whole passage, but try to avoid getting sidetracked by questions or issues that will be addressed later in the study.

8. As you ask the questions, keep in mind that they are designed to be used just as they are written. You may simply read them aloud. Or you may prefer to express them in your own words.

There may be times when it is appropriate to deviate from the study guide. For example, a question may have already been answered. If so, move on to the next question. Or someone may raise an important question not covered in the guide. Take time to discuss it, but try to keep the group from going off on tangents.

9. Avoid answering your own questions. If necessary, repeat or rephrase them until they are clearly understood. Or point out something you read in the leader's notes to clarify the context or meaning. An eager group quickly becomes passive and silent if they think the leader will do most of the talking.

10. Don't be afraid of silence. People may need time to think about the question before formulating their answers.

11. Don't be content with just one answer. Ask, "What do the rest of you think?" or "Anything else?" until several people have given answers to the question.

12. Acknowledge all contributions. Try to be affirming whenever possible. Never reject an answer. If it is clearly off-base, ask, "Which verse led you to that conclusion?" or again, "What do the rest of you think?"

13. Don't expect every answer to be addressed to you, even though this will probably happen at first. As group members become more at ease, they will begin to truly interact with each other. This is one sign of healthy discussion.

14. Don't be afraid of controversy. It can be very stimulating. If you don't resolve an issue completely, don't be frustrated. Move on and keep it in mind for later. A subsequent study may solve the problem.

15. Periodically summarize what the group has said about the passage. This helps to draw together the various ideas mentioned and gives continuity to the study. But don't preach.

16. At the end of the Bible discussion you may want to allow group members a time of quiet to work on an idea under "Now or Later." Then discuss what you experienced. Or you may want to encourage group members to work on these ideas between meetings. Give an opportunity during the session for people to talk about what they are learning.

17. Conclude your time together with conversational prayer, adapting the prayer suggestion at the end of the study to your group. Ask for God's help in following through on the commitments you've made.

18. End on time.

Many more suggestions and helps are found in *How to Lead a LifeBuilder Study*.

Components of Small Groups

A healthy small group should do more than study the Bible. There are four components to consider as you structure your time together.

Nurture. Small groups help us to grow in our knowledge and love of God. Bible study is the key to making this happen and is the foundation of your small group.

Community. Small groups are a great place to develop deep friendships with other Christians. Allow time for informal interaction before and after each study. Plan activities and games that will help you get to know each other. Spend time having fun together—going on a picnic or cooking dinner together.

Worship and prayer. Your study will be enhanced by spending time praising God together in prayer or song. Pray for each other's needs—and keep track of how God is answering prayer in your group. Ask God to help you to apply what you are learning in your study.

Outreach. Reaching out to others can be a practical way of applying what you are learning, and it will keep your group from becoming self-focused. Host a series of evangelistic discussions for your friends or neighbors. Clean up the yard of an elderly friend. Serve at a soup kitchen together, or spend a day working in the community.

Many more suggestions and helps in each of these areas are found in the *Small Group Starter Kit*. You will also find information on building a small group. Reading through the starter kit will be worth your time.

Study 1. Sunday: Triumphal Entry. Matthew 21:1-11.

Purpose: To celebrate Jesus, our humble King, and deepen our worship of him.

Question 2. The disciples might have been surprised by this request for a donkey—a humble creature—and by Jesus' detailed knowledge of where to find it. However, they also would have been aware of the Old Testament prophecy in verse 4 and may have been excited to see it fulfilled.

Question 4. According to *The NIV Study Bible,* the donkey is "symbolic of humility, peace and Davidic royalty" (p. 1469).

Question 6. Some saw Jesus as the king who would free the Jewish nation from oppression and then rule over them forever. Others saw Jesus as a prophet. However, a Jewish person would not equate the Son of David with a prophet.

Question 7. Public celebrations are great tools to draw us into worship and praise. The crowd was giving to Christ the glory due his name. In their case it was with little understanding and no heart allegiance. However, Sunday morning services and special celebrations should be helpful means to worship.

Study 2. Monday: Clearing the Temple. Mark 11:12-19.

Purpose: To better understand righteous anger and how a spirit of forgiveness is necessary when praying for God's judgment.

Group discussion. Take some notes on your discussion of the definition, and return to these ideas when you get to question 5.

Question 3. Fig trees and vines are often used as symbols of Israel's faithfulness to God. God comes to his vineyard looking for grapes and figs, that is, righteousness, justice and mercy. Thus, looking for fruit on the fig tree represents what Jesus is looking for in the temple. See, for example, Jeremiah 8:13 (RSV; NIV obscures this verse); 29:17; Hosea 9:10-16; Joel 1:7; Micah 7:1-6.

The group is apt to struggle with why Jesus curses the fig tree when "it was not the season for figs." It is probably most helpful to see this as an acted parable of the judgment that the temple faces. For those being judged, judgment seldom comes when expected.

Question 4. For the context of Jesus' comments from the Old Testament, see Isaiah 56:4-8 and Jeremiah 7:1-11.

Question 10. The withered fig tree is found in verse 20, but you may want to continue your session with this passage as it ties back into verses 12-14.

Study 3. Tuesday: Teaching at the Mount of Olives. Matthew 24:1-31.

Purpose: To consider the events preceding Christ's return and the importance of being ready for him.

Overview. In this chapter Jesus warns his followers of five dangers or difficulties they will face: (1) dependence on outward structures and systems such as the temple (vv. 1-2), (2) deception by false prophets (vv. 4-5, 11, 23, 26), (3) distraction by turmoil in the world (vv. 6-8), (4) dismay over persecution (vv. 9-13) and (5) dullness or apathy because of not knowing the day or hour of his return (vv. 36-51).

Each warning is accompanied by a promise: the temple may be destroyed, but the elect will be saved (v. 22); false prophets may appear, but the true Son of Man will come with the angels and be recognized (vv. 30-31); nations may be in turmoil, but these are the birth pangs of a new creation (v. 8); believers may be persecuted, but the faithful will be saved (v. 13); the day of his return may not be dated, but the owner will come (vv. 42-51).

Question 2. Jesus' prophecy in this chapter was prompted by the disciples' fascination with the temple in Jerusalem. It was an architectural wonder and was one of the most impressive sights in the ancient world. The rabbis said, "He who has not seen the temple in its full construction has never seen a glorious building in his life." According to Josephus, the stones of the temple were white, and some of them were thirty-seven feet long, twelve feet high and eighteen feet wide. Construction of the temple was begun by Herod the Great in 20-19 B.C. and was not fully completed until six years before the temple's destruction in A.D. 70. At that time the Roman armies under Titus actually pried the stones apart to get the gold that had melted from the gold-leafed roof during the fire. Jesus' prophecy in verse 2 was therefore literally fulfilled. For the Jews the temple was not only a great and historic building but was an assurance that God was with them. It gave them a false sense of security.

Question 3. Notice that these things are not the end (v. 6) but merely "the beginning of birth pains" (v. 8). These events will mark all of time between Jesus' first and second comings. Like birth pains, they will initially be less intense and further apart. However, as the end approaches they will increase in frequency and intensity until they culminate in the time of "great distress, unequaled from the beginning of the world until now—and never to be equaled again" (v. 21).

Question 7. Because understanding the meaning of Daniel's phrase "abomination that causes desolation" is difficult, this study does not try to unravel it. However, if the subject comes up in the study, you might suggest the following: Many scholars believe Daniel's prophecy was fulfilled in 168 B.C. when Antiochus Epiphanes erected a pagan altar to Zeus in the Jerusalem temple. Jesus' statement indicates, however, that there will be a future fulfillment of this prophecy as well. Some believe this fulfillment came with the Roman sacrilege of the temple during the destruction of Jerusalem in A.D. 70. Others think it will be fulfilled by the sacrilege of the antichrist at the end of time (2 Thess 2:4). Perhaps both are intended.

To understand the prophecy in this chapter, we need to know something about the so-called prophetic perspective. The Old Testament prophets and Jesus saw future events as we might see two distant mountain ranges. At a distance, two widely separated mountain ranges appear close together. Similarly, biblical prophecies to be fulfilled at different times often appear together in the same passage of Scripture. Jesus' prophecy in this chapter touches on two periods, the fall of Jerusalem (vv. 15-28) and the end of all things (roughly from v. 29 on).

"The elect" mentioned in verses 22, 24 and 31 are God's people (see also Mk 13:20, 22, 27; Rom 11:7; 2 Tim 2:10; Tit 1:1; 1 Pet 1:1).

Now or Later. You might choose to continue straight through the

"Now or Later" section if time allows. If so, then wait until the end to pray together.

Question 10. The lesson of the fig tree is clear enough: just as tender twigs and leaves indicate the nearness of summer, so the presence of "these things" indicate that "it" is near. But what do *these things, it* (or *he*) and *this generation* refer to? There are several possibilities. Some interpret it as the destruction of Jerusalem and therefore view "these things" as the events preceding its destruction. According to this view, *this generation* refers to the generation alive during the time of Jesus.

Others view *it* (or *he*) as the second coming of Christ, and *these things* as the events immediately preceding his return. According to this interpretation, *this generation* refers to the generation alive at the time of the second coming (or possibly to the Jewish race, since the Greek word for *generation* can mean "race"). These verses may be confusing simply because they cannot be restricted solely to one option (the fall of Jerusalem) or the other (the second coming). Perhaps there is both a more immediate fulfillment and a later fulfillment, as in the case of the "abomination that causes desolation" (see note to question 7).

Question 11. *That day* (v. 36) is one of the usual New Testament expressions for the second coming of Jesus.

Study 4. Thursday: The Last Supper. Matthew 26:17-30.

Purpose: To consider the Lord's Supper as a picture of Jesus' death on the cross and our participation in the benefits of his death.

Question 1. Notice that it is evening and Jesus is reclining at the table (they sat on the floor and used low tables, v. 20). They share a bowl (v. 23), dipping bread or meat into the sauce. So this was a full meal (v. 26), not just the bread and wine that we now have for communion.

Questions 2-3. Throughout the centuries the Passover celebration had symbolically portrayed the death of Christ, "the Lamb of God, who takes away the sin of the world" (Jn 1:29).

If the members of your group are unfamiliar with the Passover, it might be good to have them read the story in Exodus quickly and silently. However, if someone in the group can briefly summarize the significance of Passover (when it first took place, what took place and so on), that would be better.

Question 5. What were Judas's motives? None of the Gospel writers tells us, so the best we can do is reconstruct the events and conjecture about why he betrayed Jesus. We know that the religious leaders were looking for an opportunity to arrest Jesus. They wanted to do so secretly to avoid a riot during the Passover celebration in Jerusalem (Mk 14:1-2). However, because there were more than 300,000 people in the city (as opposed to its normal population of 50,000), and because Jesus had withdrawn to a village outside Jerusalem (Jn 11:54), the religious leaders had difficulty finding him (Jn 11:56). Therefore, they gave orders "that if anyone found out where Jesus was, he should report it so that they might arrest him" (Jn 11:57).

Of course Judas both knew where Jesus was and when the best opportunity would be to arrest him quietly. Therefore, he went to the chief priests and offered to hand Jesus over for thirty silver coins (Mt 26:15), about four months' wages. Why did he do it? Perhaps he was disillusioned with Jesus, who had failed to enter Jerusalem as the conquering Messiah the people expected. Perhaps Judas convinced himself that if he could not share in the messianic power and glory he had hoped for, at least he could salvage some monetary reward. Both Luke and John tell us that "Satan entered Judas" (Lk 22:3; Jn 13:27), who became a pawn in the hands of demonic powers in their attempt to destroy Jesus.

Question 7. On the relationship between God's sovereignty and human responsibility, see Acts 2:23. The Scriptures put side by side the statements about God's sovereignty and our responsibility without attempting to reconcile them.

Question 8. Jesus said, "This is my blood of the covenant, which is poured out for many for the forgiveness of sins" (v. 28). The covenant he speaks of is the New Covenant, which replaced the Old Covenant between God and Israel (Ex 24:8). The prophet Jeremiah spoke of a day when God would establish this New Covenant: "'The time is coming,' declares the LORD, 'when I will make a new covenant with the house of Israel and with the house of Judah. It will not be like the covenant I made with their forefathers when I took them by the hand to lead them out of Egypt, because they broke my covenant, though I was a husband to them,' declares the LORD" (Jer 31:31-32). (See also Heb 8:6-13.)

Question 9. Obviously we must interpret the Lord's Supper in light of further New Testament revelation. The event itself only gives us a glimpse and a picture of truths explained much more fully later on. However, it is significant that the symbolism involves not only the bread and wine—pictures of Christ's body and blood—but also the eating and drinking of these elements by his followers. In other words, we must somehow intimately partake of Christ's death in order to participate in its benefits. Eating the bread and drinking the wine, therefore, become symbols of saving faith (see Jn 6:53-63).

Question 12. Matthew tells us that the perfume was "very expensive" (v. 7). Mark 14:5 says it was worth more than a year's wages (300 denarii).

Jesus' statement about the poor always being with us (v. 11) has been twisted to mean that we should not do anything to try to eliminate poverty. It becomes a rationalization not to help. But clearly Jesus' intention is to indicate that there is always an opportunity and an obligation to help those in poverty.

Question 13. How is love's extravagance justified? (1) By the beauty of her devotion. (2) By an opportunity that will not always be there. (3) By the ability of the devotee—"she did what she could" (Mk 14:8). (4) And by the spiritual significance of an occasion—in this case Jesus' burial—that has out-of-the-ordinary meaning.

Study 5. Thursday: Betrayal & Arrest. Mark 14:43-72.

Purpose: To explore the variety of motives involved in Jesus' betrayal and abandonment, and to draw warnings and encouragement for times of our own testing as disciples.

Question 4. In trying to save himself, the young man loses what little he has. Some have thought this young man was Mark himself, included anonymously in this account of Jesus' betrayal.

Question 6. In identifying himself as the Christ, Jesus goes on to link himself with "the Son of Man" described in Daniel 7:13-14. This is the first time his public use of the title "Son of Man" would have had clear messianic overtones.

Jesus has used the phrase "Son of Man" four times so far (2:10, 28; 8:31, 38). With hindsight it is rather easy to see that Jesus was speaking about himself and alluding to his role as Messiah. Jesus' hearers, however, would not likely have heard him that way. To them the phrase "Son of Man" would likely have sounded like another way of saying *man* (as in Ps 8:4, where it means just that). I. Howard Marshall explains, "It can be used to refer both to the humanity of Jesus and also to his divine origin. Jesus can use the term to refer to himself as a human over against God (Mk 2:10, 28), but also to indicate divine origin. In the latter case 'Son of man' is a veiled way of expressing his relationship to God" (*Dictionary of Jesus and the Gospels* [Downers Grove, Ill.: InterVarsity Press, 1992], pp. 780-81). Further insights into Jesus' use of "Son of Man" can be found in Mark 9:9, 12, 31; 10:33, 13:26; 14:21, 41.

Question 7. The issue here is that if Jesus was not God, he was clearly guilty of blasphemy.

Study 6. Friday: Trial. John 18:28—19:16.

Purpose: To demonstrate that even though Jesus was crucified unjustly, he willingly submitted to death for our sins, providing forgiveness and a model of grace for our lives.

Question 1. Pontius Pilate was a Roman career bureaucrat about the same age as Jesus. His official title was procurator of Judea. He came to Judea in A.D. 26, hoping that he would soon be promoted to a more civilized section of the empire. From the moment he arrived in Judea, however, everything went wrong. After two or three major political blunders, Pilate found himself at the mercy of the Jewish leaders. They knew that enough pressure would make Pilate do whatever they asked.

Jesus' final religious trial had been held in the temple area before the Sanhedrin, the Jewish supreme court. Right next to the temple was the Roman fortress of Antonia. The Roman army was stationed there and Pilate, the governor, lived there. So it required just a very short walk to take Jesus to the civil authority for final condemnation.

Question 2. According to *The NIV Study Bible:* "The chief priests evidently held a second session of the Sanhedrin after daybreak to give some appearance of legality to what they did (Mk 15:1). This occasion would have been immediately after that, perhaps between 6:00 A.M. and 7:00 A.M" (p. 1632). Entering a Gentile home would have made them unclean.

Question 5. See 18:39; 19:4, 6, 10, 12, 15.

Question 9. If conversation lags, follow up with, "Shouldn't he have defended himself more vigorously?"

Study 7. Friday: Crucifixion. Matthew 27.

Purpose: To consider the mysterious triumph of the kingdom of heaven through the suffering and death of Jesus on the cross.

Question 1. This is a grim chapter. Jesus is killed. It appears that evil will triumph. Both the international authorities (the Romans) and the local authorities (the Jewish leaders) participate in Jesus' death. You may discover that there is a sense of letdown as you finish the study. This is to be expected. We all need to look at the terrible reality of the death of Jesus at the hands of humankind. After you finish the study, encourage people to look forward to the last chapter, the resurrection.

Question 2. It is obvious that Jesus' message has gotten through, and people now know what he teaches. Those who mock him demonstrate that they just do not believe him. Jesus is mocked for saying that he is a king, that he can raise up the temple of God, that he is the Son of God and that he has come to save Israel. If he dies (and stays dead), then obviously all these statements are indeed false and Jesus will be shown to be a fake.

Question 3. There is a disruption in the Trinity that has effects through all of creation. Jesus is quoting Psalm 22:1 which reads, "My God, my God, why have you forsaken me? Why are you so far from saving me, so far from the words of my groaning?"

Question 6. Most of Jesus' followers were not present. However, the women watched from a distance. Joseph was also courageous in asking for the body of Jesus. Some of the emotions they might have felt were sadness, responsibility, loyalty, love, care and pain.

Question 10. This question is not meant to be guilt-inducing. Sometimes we are in a situation of pain and suffering that we must give to God again and again. This doesn't mean that we don't have faith. It's part of the process of finding hope in God.

Study 8. Sunday: Resurrection. Luke 24:1-43.

Purpose: To celebrate the truth of the resurrection and to discover how it shapes our lives.

Question 1. Notice that the actions of those who visited the tomb are psychologically credible.

Question 2. Luke mentions the women because they were actually the first at the tomb. If this were not true, no Gospel writer would have invented it for the purposes of testimony. The notice of their presence helps establish the credibility of the account.

If discussion about whether the women went to the wrong tomb should arise, point the group to Luke 23:55-56. The women had seen where he was buried.

Question 7. Jesus wants his disciples to know who he is and that what he has done is a fulfillment of prophecy. The disciples will be witnesses to what has occurred, and it is implied, when they are "clothed with power from on high" they "will preach repentance and forgiveness of sins" from Jerusalem to all nations (Lk 24:45-49).

Question 9. It is important to note that Jesus is not a "ghost" (Lk 24:37) but the same person as the one crucified. His body is no longer in the tomb; it has been transmuted, but it is in some ways the same body.

The evidence for the resurrection is of six types, five of which we have noted already: (1) the empty tomb (the body is gone), (2) the position of the graveclothes, (3) the postresurrection appearance of Jesus to his followers, (4) the fulfillment of his prophecy prior to his death, and (5) the consistency of the resurrection with his other claims. A fuller study of the New Testament would include a major additional item: (6) the change of the disciples from weak individuals to strong leaders willing to undergo persecution and death for their belief in Jesus and his resurrection. (Tradition says most of them died as martyrs.)

Cindy Bunch is associate publisher and director of editorial at InterVarsity Press. She is also the author and coauthor of several LifeBuilder Bible Studies, including Christian Virtues *and* Woman of God.